Is That Your Mother Calling?

Advice that Echoes Down Through the Ages

Marlis Manley

Dedication

For Linda, Nancy, Steve, and Emily.

Marlis Manley

In memory of my grandmother, Nettie Marie Hart Cook.

After I explained to some friends how, as a young girl, she would kill a live chicken and fry it up for her and her six siblings' school lunches—she said, "Well, you can't kill a dead chicken."

Acknowledgment

With deep gratitude to the people of Iowa State University who, in the mid-1980s, graciously shared words of advice that had stayed with them down through the years. Each might justifiably have entreated, along with survey respondent C.N.--

"There are bits of me entrusted to you in here; treat me gently, please."

Marlis Manley

CONTENTS

Marlis Manley

Forewarned

When was the last time you found yourself nagged by a familiar voice reverberating in your head as you were about to fang into that slice of Death-by-Chocolate cake, get a tattoo, or rekindle a love affair that went down years ago in the blistering flames of family disapproval?

A friend of mine confessed she hadn't taken a bite of dessert in years without recalling the caution, "A moment on the lips; a lifetime on the hips." And that was second-hand advice once removed: something she'd read in *People Magazine* that had been passed down to an actress by her mother. That hasn't actually resulted in my friend changing her eating habits, but to hear her tell it, it can take the shine off the hot fudge.

As far as words of wisdom go, some are more helpful than others. The best advice I've received? "When facing a loss, focus on whatever remains and count it as a gain because you could have lost everything." The worst? When I was a freshman in college and took creative writing classes, a family member remarked, "Well, you can't be a writer."

And I got it—no one was knocking down the door asking for an 18-year-old midwestern, middle-class girl's thoughts on the human condition. (Obviously, I soldiered on; for me, it wasn't a matter of choice.)

The following words of wisdom, platitudes, and some fairly random advice were shared with people born between 1926 and 1968. I can guarantee some of it will be familiar. For example, the admonition to wear clean underwear "in case you're in an accident" rings loud and clear through every generation. Other bits of advice are sure to be a surprise (see Part Four: Say What?).

One irrefutable truth is apparent—there is a deep-rooted desire in each generation to decode the world as they've experienced it for the following generations. Their efforts range from profound to poignant to puzzling (I guess you had to be there), and some of it is just plain hilarious. And sometimes, there are long-lived consequences.

–From a female respondent, born in 1960 – *What a fascinating project! My family is generally programmed to give advice CONSTANTLY—warranted or otherwise.*

Part One: Advice on Dating and Marriage

"If a marriage is on the rocks,

the rocks are in the bed."

Is That Your Mother Calling?

Female, born 1943, from Grandmother…

"If a marriage is on the rocks, the rocks are in the bed."

"I was amazed to find her so open about sex. And also, somewhat surprisingly,"--

"Let parents pick your spouse."

"My grandmother's parents picked her husband for her, someone of the same religion who looked to be a 'good provider.' However, after 50 years of marriage and nine kids, my grandmother would still tell us she liked 'X' better but couldn't have married him because he was a Catholic."

[Editor's note: No rocks in that bed, apparently. But I do wonder how many more kids there might have been had she married the Catholic.)

Marlis Manley

Female, born 1926, from Mother...

"You know, if you don't find a husband in college, you probably never will."

"I had come home on vacation my senior year of college, and we were waiting for a bus to take us shopping. It reinforced my own fears that I was never going to find a suitable husband, and in 1949, this branded me as an 'old maid.' Subconsciously, she made me focus more on husband hunting than on developing myself for an independent life.

I can laugh at it now, but it adds to my resentment that my mother fostered a dependent attitude in me at a time when I was struggling to face the world alone. I would rather have been encouraged to educate myself for my own goals, and if a marriage happened, so much the better.

I did find a suitable husband and have had a happy marriage, family, and—later in life—career. However, I do wonder what paths my life might have taken me if I had been more secure in my ability to pursue some of my interests in the 'great unknown' without the support and protection of a husband."

[Editor's note: I overheard my mother telling my aunt they were sending me to college to find a husband with potential. I did find a good starter husband and great breeder (we had three choice kiddos). Then I returned to grad school and found another one, my English professor. So, I guess you could say it worked for me.]

Female, born 1926, from Mother...

"Don't go out with a married man. If he'll cheat on his wife, he'll cheat on you."

"It was good advice and basically true. I never followed it, but really never had to pay the price."

[Editor's note: Perhaps because forewarned is forearmed?]

Female, born 1968, from Father, after her sister's wedding...

"The real marriage starts after the honeymoon."

"I thought it was just because he thought my sister might have approached the marriage with some false perceptions. With increased knowledge and after listening to my sister, I tend to believe what he said. My perception of marriage has changed, and I wonder how this will affect my own choice."

Female, born 1969, from Mother, when the girl wanted to date at 14…

"Don't date too soon. Try and wait until you're 18."

"I thought the idea was pretty stupid and sounded silly. Even when I look back on it, I find it amusing. I went out on the date anyway and have been dating since."

Female, born 1924, from Father, upon her engagement…

"Don't marry a man who is 27 years older, a foreigner with a past but no future [because he was a refugee]. One problem alone can break a marriage; you will have three problems to deal with."

"I had to prove I could act independently at 21 and was sure true love would take care of all the problems. Today, I think even I would give the same advice as my father for good reasons—but there are always exceptions. It was not an easy marriage, but I would do it again, even knowing what the future would bring."

Marlis Manley

Male, born 1968, from a friend...

"Why have the main course when you can have the smorgasbord?"

"When my friend told me his views on getting married, I thought it was funny, but later I felt sorry for him. He's the type of person most likely to get divorced, while I value my relationships."

Female, born 1966, from Mother...

"Hickeys are a sign of heavy petting."

"I was so embarrassed. Now I think it was funny—but I didn't let my fiancé put them on my neck anymore."

Female, born 1945, from Mother…

"In a marriage, love and friendship are equally important. Love may pass, but friendship will stay."

"Mom told me this the first time one of my classmates told me I was pretty and he wanted to marry me. I was SIX YEARS OLD! Early on, I thought love would never end, but what my mother told me is absolutely true. I have approached my loving relationships and marriage keeping that in mind."

[Editor's note: At six, I was warned to stop stepping on the heels of my mother's penny loafers as a "joke."]

Female, born 1944, from Mother during high school…

"Stay away from Greg."

"I felt resentment. I'm sorry I listened. I'm single; he's a priest."

Also from Mother…

"You need to have a career before you get married."

"She tried to warn me when I got engaged. It was actually good advice. Unfortunately, her prediction proved true."

Female, born 1923, from Mother when a girl was planning to get married...

"Marriage should be a partnership."

"I wondered why she said "should," then realized she didn't feel her marriage was a partnership. My dad was the head of the household the way her father had been. And Dad was a good one, so I grew up thinking the man should be. However, I thought I could carry her advice into my marriage and be more of a partner.

If my husband hadn't died very young, so I was forced to take over the responsibilities of both parents for three children (one not yet born when he died), I think I would still have deferred to him in most decisions, but I was still much more of a partner than our mothers were in their marriages.

Once I had to become the 'head' without wanting to be, my

father's 'Be tough' advice helped me through. By the time I remarried eight years later, my new husband knew while we were dating that this had to be a true partnership (he has been a wonderful partner)."

Female, born 1945, from Mother, consistently…

"Get married. A woman needs a man."

"I generally disregarded it as it made me mad, and I felt the same about it over the years. I'm still single."

Female, born 1954, from Father…

"Once you're married, you're going to have to wake up with that very same person every day."

"When I was in an unhappy relationship during college with

someone and felt trapped, my dad suggested I ride with him to the bakery for bread, and that was when he made me think about what the future might look like. I thought my dad was both sensitive and brilliant. I didn't marry the schmuck."

Female, born 1948, from Mother...

"If you marry someone rich, you earn it."

"She said this as I was about to divorce a rich man, and I thought she was right on target. I still laugh when friends or family talk about wanting rich relatives."

Female, born 1960, from Father...

"Keep your jeans up."

"When I was dating and contemplating marriage, I thought

it was funny his two rules were to choose someone from a good family and keep my 'jeans' up."

Female, born 1948, from Father...

"Just remember, when you get married, you are marrying the whole family. Take a good look at them, and see if that's what you want."

"This was shortly before I was married, and I thought it was kind of silly because I didn't think I'd be around his family that much. I wish I'd listened to my father. My husband turned out a lot like them, and we ended up divorced seven years later with three children. I raised the children alone and still have to associate with his family. There has been a lot of hurt and sadness over the years because of the marriage."

Female, born 1952, from Mother and Father...

"You made your bed. Now lie in it."

"I wasn't getting along with my spouse after my parents had advised me not to marry him. I went ahead and got a divorce, and I think I did the right thing."

Female, born 1961, from Mother

"I'd rather have you on the pill than pregnant."

"I was in junior high school and was casually seeing a man five years older than I. I admired my mother for having that attitude. She could have just said to me, 'You'd better not be sleeping with him,' but instead, she was realistic about the situation. I wasn't anyway, but I went on the pill soon after that and just had my first child nine-and-a-half years later and after three years of marriage."

Female, born 1961, from Mother and Father, on separate occasions…

"Don't be picky. Go out with anyone who asks."

"This was before I went off to college, and I thought, okay, sure, but it was bad advice for me because it led to a lot of dates with guys I wasn't interested in, so they were bad dates. It might be good advice regarding guys within your own social circle with whom you are already friendly, but not with any Tom, Dick, or Harry. Now, I hate dating in general and have vowed not to go out with anyone unless I really like him. I'm sick of bad dates."

Female, born 1967, from Father…

"Girls shouldn't date until age 18."

"I thought it was okay because I wasn't interested in dating, but later, I realized I should have been allowed to have more early experience dating because now I can't feel comfortable around dates."

Male, born 1968, from his friend…

"Beauty is altogether in the eye of the beholder."

"My friend said that to me about a girl I was getting all hot about, and I didn't really appreciate it. Later, I realized it doesn't matter what people look like on the outside as much as what they're like on the inside, as a person."

Female, born 1966, from mother…

"Never have kids."

"After a fiery argument between my 13-year-old brother and 11-year-old sister, my mom said that to me, and I wished she'd thought of that 13 years earlier. I realized she made the comment in the midst of frustration, but I did decide not to have children until I was mature enough to handle the responsibility of raising them."

Male, born 1966, from Father…

"If you do it, you'd better take precautions."

"I was just hitting puberty, hadn't started dating, and I was mostly embarrassed that he thought I was that stupid. Of course, it was very good advice. I'm still single and childless."

"I know you think you just want to date him, but there's always that first date with the man you will eventually marry."

"My mother reminded me of this when I dated someone she did not approve of, usually someone of a different religion. I didn't think much of it, and I still don't. I had four daughters and made sure I never conveyed that message to them.

"It's better to discuss these things in person. Don't write anything down that you don't want to come back and haunt you."

"That was what she told me when I was breaking up with a boyfriend, and I thought it was good advice, but I felt I just had to write the letter anyway."

[Editor's note: No point telling this to kids in the age of the Internet. There's more dirty laundry hanging out here than you can shake a stain-remover stick at.]

Male, born 1946, from a family friend considered an 'uncle'...

"When you get the urge, don't get married. Go somewhere professionals will take care of you."

"Uncle had just had a fight with his wife, and I was getting a view—at age 13—of how grim adult life could be. Now, I think Uncle was irresponsible, and it contributed to my having difficulty in forming reliable impressions of people.

Male, born 1944, to his son and daughter-in-law…

"Marriage isn't so much work as it is communication."

"I remind them of this regularly because it's advice I wish someone had given to me prior to my failed marriage. Now, I attempt to practice it in any serious relationship, regardless of whether it's with a spouse, a friend, or a member of the family. I've found relationships stay healthier and stronger as long as communication occurs."

Female, born 1926, from mother…

"I pity the man who marries you."

"My mother said this when I didn't keep my room clean, and for a time, I thought I might honestly never marry. Blarney! I've been married to the same man for 40 years. (And he is not to be pitied.) That remark has probably shaped my rebellion against 'keeping an immaculate house' as my mother did. My own children were subjected to a much more casual home environment as they were growing up.

To a man, born 1934, from Father…

"Don't be in such a hurry. If she's the right woman, she is worth waiting for. If not, you won't have to live with her so long."

"Dad suspected I was dating the wrong girl, but I thought he just didn't understand. Actually, he knew more than I did. I met and married the right one the next year."

Part Two: Advice to Young Men

"Big boys don't cry."

Marlis Manley

Born 1938, from Mother...

"Big boys don't cry."

"She said it when I'd had minor hurts mostly, but after some psychological hurts as well. I found it frustrating and even demeaning. I think that kind of expectation put on boys can lead to male insensitivity."

[Editor's note: I think psychologists and educators have begun to agree with him. See below.]

Born 1965, from Mother...

"It's okay for boys to cry."

"Early in high school, I had a date broken by a girl, and it hit me hard. I knew Mom meant well, but I felt guilty for crying.

While it's good in practice, I still feel socialized to control my emotions. If her advice had any effect, maybe it was to make me feel more androgynous."

Born 1969, from Father…

"Girls will play games and try to use you. Watch them closely. Make sure you know which one you really like."

"We were having a little father-son talk, and it sounded like good advice to me then and even now. I've been paying close attention to girls since—I keep a good eye on them."

[Editor's note: Does anyone else sense a double entendre here?]

Marlis Manley

Born 1951, from Father…

"Busy people are happy people."

"Whenever I looked bored, or at the other extreme, felt overwhelmingly busy, my dad would say this. Now that I'm older, in my opinion, busyness or productivity isn't necessarily a measure of happiness. Other criteria are more important for assessing one's happiness. Yet it's difficult for me not to feel guilty when I'm relaxing or being "unproductive.""

Born 1949, from Mother…

"Make sure you have a clean handkerchief and underwear—in case you're run over by a bus."

"Seems like I heard this every time I went outside. Back then, it struck fear into me. When I got older, I considered it hogwash, but every now and then, I wonder what kind of mess would await my next of kin should I 'check out.'"

[Editor's note: I love the specificity of the "embarrassment by bus."]

Born 1949, from Father...

"Real men don't resort to the use of profanity."

"This was the response when I reported on what I'd heard at school or a friend's house. I thought it would be both nice and yet horrible to be above it all like my father. And I thought he could have made his point without the use of a categorical statement. As a result, I always feel as though I am on the outside, looking in. I'm too intense to avoid using the language my father prohibited but too much of a boy scout to enjoy it."

Born 1935, from his pastor…

"Be as meek as a sheep and wise as a fox when dealing with groups of people."

"He was sharing a lesson in strategy, and I thought it was good advice. Over the years, it's helped me a lot in dealing with committees and administrative groups."

Born 1927, from Mother…

"It is easier to say no over the phone than it is to say it face to face."

"It was the first time I was contemplating asking a girl for a date to go to a movie. I knew it was good advice, but I was pretty apprehensive about meeting a girl in private and asking. I have been in a position from time to time where I have needed assistance or been trying to sell something, and that advice has stood me in good stead."

Born 1927, from Father...

"Don't measure a man by where he is but by how far he has come."

"He said this sometime during my adolescence, and while I knew it was something important, I was a bit perplexed about its application. Over the years, it has been of great help to me in understanding people from various social stations. It has helped me to be at peace with them, with myself, and with my father."

Born 1938, from Father...

"Can't never did anything."

"I heard that any and every time I was uncertain about taking a risk or trying something new and said, "But I can't do that." He usually convinced me I might as well try. Later, it became, "We'll give it the old college try, and I guess someone will tell us if we're doing it wrong."

Born 1946, from Father…

"I can't say I like your fighting with your sisters and brothers, but if you must do it, do it at home. Outside this house, you are a family, and I expect you to support each other without reservation."

"This came up on several occasions, especially when I was in my teens. I remember realizing it was a good policy but not receiving it gracefully. I tell my children the same thing. And I do not speak ill of my family no matter how much they may deserve it at times."

Born 1946, from Mother…

"Treat books with respect. You can own nothing more valuable than a book."

"It seems like I heard this every day of my life as a child. We had hundreds of books, and they were always being read and scattered about. It was excellent advice. Now I'm a professor and probably spend more time reading and writing than any other activity."

Born 1934, from Father…

"You are old enough to know right from wrong. If you get into trouble, you can get out the same way you got in—by yourself."

"I knew he meant it. He was an alderman, and he wanted me to know where he stood: no special favors. He was right, and

I make sure I'm responsible for what I do."

Born 1943, from Father, a physician…

"These patients are in the hospital because they're sick."

"I was working as an orderly in a hospital and complained about the grumpiness and ingratitude the patients expressed. He was telling me to quit complaining, but I also took it to mean, 'If you can't take the heat, get out of the kitchen.' I got into a profession where no one is grumpy or lacks gratitude."

[Editor's note: I wish I'd thought to ask him what he ended up doing.]

Born 1946, from Father…

"Don't act like you've never been anywhere."

"When we were going into a public place, and I was horsing around, he didn't want me to embarrass the family. (Back then, I hadn't been anywhere.) I ended up with some general self-consciousness."

Born 1964, from Father...

"Every generation must rebuild the wheel."

"After I had been through a real bad time in my life, I think he actually said this for his benefit as well. All during my plunge into the worst experience of my life, Dad kept trying to warn me I was making a big mistake. But I did it anyway. Now, I know it couldn't be more true.

As I see my sister growing up, I realize teens will be teens. I think about telling her of my experience in the hopes she will learn from me and not make the same mistakes, but that's not possible.

Should I ever have children, I hope I would raise them with no question in my mind that I did my best, and when they got to the rebellious stage, I would give them something to think about, but most importantly, I would be there for them and listen to their needs, knowing in my heart they have to learn from their own mistakes and not from mine."

Born 1967 from his parents…

"The world doesn't revolve around you."

"Whenever I was being selfish, they'd remind me of this. I thought they were crazy, but as I got older, I found they were right. Accepting it has meant I can deal and get along better with other people."

[Editor's note: I don't recall my complaint, but my grandmother's response was, "You know, Marlis, the whole world can't be out of step. Maybe it's you." Boom]

Born 1942, from Mother…

"Don't smoke. It will stunt your growth."

"That scared me because, unbeknownst to her, I'd tried a cigarette butt I'd found along the road. I was six or seven and cried because I thought I'd never grow up. To this day, I don't smoke."

[Editor's note: Unbeknownst? I'd bet dollars to donuts Mom had an inkling.]

Born 1961, from Mother…

"Never call in sick (to school, work, etc.) on a Monday or a Friday."

"Every time a co-worker is sick on a Monday or Friday, I remember what Mom said about people thinking they were taking an extended weekend or recovering from a drunk one."

Born 1962, from Mother and Grandfather...

"If you don't have a good head, you'd better have good legs."

"Whenever I forgot an item, my mom had sent me to the downstairs cupboard to get, and I'd have to make another trip, they'd say it. Now I say it to myself nearly every day."

[Editor's note: As do I, sadly.]

Born 1943, from his college instructor...

"Never be satisfied with a Gentleman C."

"He said this during a lecture, and what I heard was I

personally needed to work harder and put out my best effort all the time. This resulted in some significant accomplishments later on."

Born 1930, from Grandfather...

"Learn to accept, without complaining, events in your life you have no control over."

"When I was eleven years old, and a hail storm wiped out his crop, he said, 'Well, maybe we'll have a crop next year.' I was deeply impressed and have tried to apply his philosophy to my life."

Born 1930, from Father...

"I'll tell you the same as my father told me—if you want to smoke, come to me, and I'll give you everything you need, but I'd better never catch you trying it out behind

the barn.”

“This was when some of my friends were starting to smoke. I figured I'd better not do it. I thought he handled the situation well, and neither of us ever smoked, though my grandfather smoked a pipe.”

Born 1951, from Mother…

“If one does it, you all get the punishment; that way, I'll know I've got the right one! (In a family of five brothers and two sisters.)”

“When three of my brothers learned to ride the neighbor's bike and rode it on the highway, my mother walked from our farm to the neighbors' and spanked all of us. When she grabbed me, I said, 'But I don't even know how to ride a bike,' and she said, 'Someday you will, and you'll remember this.' She was right; I've never forgotten it. I was in college before I rode a bike on a public street or highway. She used this method especially when we told on one another, and that taught us to work out our own problems without fighting, which was punishable."

Born 1951, from Father...

"Just remember, the millstone of life grinds slowly, but it grinds fine."

"My father dropped this on me when I was a college sophomore leaving for spring break in Florida. I pondered that one the entire trip down with my friends. It sort of put an ominous cloud over the proceedings. When I think of taking time off work and enjoying myself, that memory often comes up. He instilled a strong work ethic, but I continue to try to find balance in my life."

Born 1930, from Grandfather...

"Only those who never attempt to do something never run risks, never fail."

"I was feeling depressed, and this made a lot of sense to me. He convinced me I should not fear failure and just keep trying and improving what I'm doing. That's why I became a researcher."

Born 1933, from Father...

"Only advice about sex: 'You probably know about girls; well, I can tell you where to get rubbers by the gross. Of course, you have to roll them yourself.'"

"This was before I was married, and I found it funny to get that kind of advice from my father, but at least he tried. And it was practical advice, but I never followed it."

[Editor's note: Roll them?]

Born 1933, from Mother...

"Clean your plate; others are hungry.'"

"I heard this many mealtimes during World War II, and I still practice it, which is why I have this spare tire around my middle."

Born 1933, from Grandfather...

"You'll never know what she'll say if you don't ask her.'"

"I heard it a lot in my youth and early teen years. I didn't think much of it then, but later realized it's fantastic advice when you think of the missed opportunities and experiences that result in the failure to ask. I think I've had a much fuller life, with many opportunities not missed."

Born 1945, from Father…

"When you're attacked in some manner by one you love, it may be only that they feel threatened by a force they cannot control and that you are a "safe" target against whom they can vent frustration.'"

"My cat was being chased by an eager animal, and when my father, of whom the cat was quite fond, let him into the porch as an escape route, the cat turned around and bit my father on the leg.

I was dumbstruck the cat would do that to a person who had always been kind to him, and I thought my father showed a great deal of understanding, even in his pain. As I get older, I marvel more and more at my father's insight. When I'm attacked verbally or otherwise, I first try to assess if that person feels threatened and I'm not actually their source of frustration."

[Editor's note: This is probably a safer bet with people you aren't married to.]

Born 1959, from his aunt (legal guardian)...

"Football is too rough; you could get hurt, so you can't go out for it."

"I was in the eighth grade when they'd started wearing pads, and I thought she was being silly because I played all the time with the neighborhood kids, who were already in high school, and we never used pads or helmets. She let me go out for varsity baseball because then I *couldn't get hurt.*' So, in the first game, I slid into second base, broke both bones in my leg, and cracked my ankle. I was in the hospital for a week and a cast for three months. Actually, football is rough, and I will probably steer my children toward a different sport."

Born 1942, from Mother...

"It won't make a difference a hundred years from now."

"I was overly concerned with having the *'right'* clothes to wear, and I would hear this when my siblings and I were concerned about making a good impression. I thought it was an excuse for not having what we thought of as *'fine'* and *'correct.'* I'm still too serious about myself and the impression I make, but I am improving. I like to think about people who lived a hundred years ago and wonder what their concerns were. I'm trying to see myself in the overall scheme of life rather as the center."

Born 1925, from Mother...

"You can be anything you want to be."

"She repeated this in my teens often, and I thought, 'Well,

maybe,' but now I realize there are such things as genetic limitations that were unknown to her."

Born 1931, from Father...

"It's not what you know in this world that counts. It's who you know."

"This came up in family discussions, and I believed it was excellent advice. As I get older, I see how true it is."

[Editor's Note: When my birth father said this, I, as a teenager, was indignant at the prospect of glomming on to someone just because she had influence—and equally daunted by the realization I was never likely to know anyone like that.]

Born 1930, from Father...

"You are the architect of your own destiny, and don't blame others for your own failures; just work harder, that's all."

"He told me this when I was depressed because things were not working as expected, and I was blaming everything and everybody. It made sense to me, and I thought, 'My father is right again.' It taught me to be a lot more disciplined."

Born 1935 from his sister (five years older)...

"John, you are so dumb."

"Usually, when I missed or ignored instructions, asking *'Why'* innocently. I usually laughed because she would laugh almost convulsively as she said it. It might have been a sibling jealousy response because I know now that she felt displaced and even rejected when I was born. One result was that I was never a confident person. Not until my oldest daughter graduated high school in the top two-and-a-half percent of her class did I ever question my sister's statement.

When I wrote about my daughter, my sister's response to my mother was, 'I just don't understand. I was the smart one, and John was the dumb one, but his children all do so well, and mine just get by.' When my mother told me this in my wife's presence, I laughed, but my wife was outraged. Out of my mother's presence, my wife asked, "Which of you had the higher school average?' I told her I did, but only because I set out to beat my sister my last two years. In short, I never questioned I was the dumb one, but a second result is that I will do what I set out to do, no matter how much time and energy it takes."

Born 1956, from Mother…

"You'll never be able to afford children, so have them now."

"This was when we were deciding about starting a family and kept thinking of postponing until we felt we could afford children. I thought Mom's response was kind of backward. Children are expensive. We now have three."

[Editor's note: She wouldn't be the first mom to lobby for getting grandchildren sooner rather than later.]

Born 1956, from Father...

"Never back up farther than necessary."

"When I was learning to drive, my dad cautioned me about avoiding backing up. I guess it makes sense. I've never backed into anything. I've given my wife the same advice, and I'm sure I'll tell my kids the same."

Born 1931, from his gunny sergeant…

"Thirty years from now, no one will know the difference."

"In Korea, when I was in a difficult field situation, his advice helped me keep perspective."

Part Three: Advice to Young Women

"You can never mend a

broken reputation."

Marlis Manley

"You can never mend a broken reputation."

"We were washing dishes when she brought it up, and it scared me. Not only did I believe her, I wondered if I could lose my reputation unknowingly. Now I see it as too extreme—really a veiled threat!"

"Keep your zipper up."

"That was his advice upon learning I was living with two of my male friends. I thought he was being ridiculous because they were my best friends, not my lovers. He understands finally they are only friends, but only because I constantly remind him."

Born 1952, from Mother...

"Remember, not everyone can be the winner."

"This was during several competitions I was in during high school. I thought it was a rotten thing to say to your child. It definitely gave me a feeling of inferiority."

Born 1952, from Grandmother...

"Women are stronger than men and can stand more."

"She told me this several times during my childhood, and I believed her, then and now. I prefer to work with women."

Born 1967, from Mother...

"You have to lie down to be a doormat."

"Mom told me this whenever she thought my friends were using me. At the time, I thought she was being strange. Of course, I wouldn't let people use me! Let alone that they ever would. So I thought. Now I think it's some of the best advice I've ever received. I don't 'lie down' anymore."

Born 1944, from Mother…

"You need to dress better. Wear dresses."

"Mom brought it up whenever she could. She didn't understand then, and I continued to resist. She's beginning to understand better.

Born 1926 from Father…

"She can do anything she wants."

"My father expressed faith in my ability many times. It made me feel 10 feet tall. I honestly believed there was nothing I couldn't tackle. What a wonderful feeling to have the most important person in your life believe in you. It helped me succeed academically—I got my doctorate. Even now, I feel that very little is beyond my reach if I really set my heart on doing something."

Born 1968, from Mother...

"Just wait until you're a mom."

"When I complained about rules or told her I'd never say or do this or that when I was a mom, she'd tell me to write down what I'd never do and look at it later and laugh. I thought I'd never be like her with all those rules, that I would remember and not say such and such to my kids. Somehow, as you get older, your mom gets smarter—funny how that works. My mom was great and knew what she was doing (most of the time). I'll be a mom just like her."

Born 1933, from Mother…

"Be sweet."

"Leaving for school or any other occasion when I was saying goodbye, she'd always remind me. I hated it. I was not, never will be, 'sweet.' To this day, I resent being told that."

Born 1965, from Mother and Father…

"You can't make someone love you."

"While I was in a relationship that I wanted badly to work out but knew was breaking up, they tried to caution me. I knew they were right, but I had to try anyway. Now I can see it the way they did, and I'll probably share this advice with my children if need be."

Born 1949, from Father...

"The fruit doesn't fall far from the tree —meaning off-spring often exhibit attitudes and behaviors similar to their parents'. It was a way for my father to explain all sorts of 'value' questions I had about relationships, social behavior, etc."

"I thought it was the gospel, and he was always right. When I got older, I realized such judgments don't always give a person a chance to be seen as an individual in his or her own right. It took me a long time to get over categorizing people by what I knew about their parents."

Born 1968, from Grandmother...

"Time is precious."

"We were on a trip to Europe together, and it made me

realize how important time really is—being with my grandmother and listening to all of her stories about her life and experiences. I think I make the most out of each of my important experiences. I want to have stories to tell my children about my life."

Born 1968, from Mother...

"You have to suffer to be beautiful."

"Whenever I complained while dressing up in something like tight shoes or nylons or taking time to have nice nails and hair or going to the dermatologist or not being able to eat junky food, she'd remind me. I knew it was true and that I'd have to settle for 'suffering.' I say it sarcastically now when I have to try to look good, and I envy guys who usually don't do anything. What women go through …. You have to try your best and laugh at yourself along the way."

Born 1942, from Mother and Father...

"It's important to be aware of good hygiene practices— ironed clothes and a neat appearance."

"Mother also harped about good posture, and I walked around with a book on my head to straighten up. I thought they overdid the posture bit, but I agreed with all the other areas. Now, I'm a beauty consultant, so I feel personal appearance and make-up are important, and I'm into accessories and jewelry. I love helping women make themselves more attractive."

Born 1942, from Mother...

"When they're talking about me, they're letting someone else rest."

"She said this when anyone felt someone might be gossiping

about them. I thought it was helpful because it makes light of gossip and makes you feel that it's wasting time and non-productive to give time to wondering what other people are saying about you."

[Editor's note: My grandmother said we'd worry less about what others think of us if we realized how seldom they do. She had a lot of dropped-mic moments.]

Born 1949, from Mother...

"Men like a woman to have an air of mystery."

"Mom said. I did this when I was a teen, and even then, I thought men should prefer openness and honesty. Today, I would express it differently, but I do think men who stay in love with one woman do so because there is something about her that is not possessable. I think this is compatible with openness and honesty and amounts more to her having a basic sense of self-worth and independence."

Born 1945, from Mother...

"Women should not intrude in men's affairs or be 'pushy.'"

"I accepted it as the way things were. My mother lived by that and criticized women who were pushy. I now think it was bad advice. I have those 'pushy' instincts and vacillate between being assertive and passive. And although my parents are proud of my achievements and roles (I work in Agriculture Administration), I sense their disapproval when they perceive me being assertive."

Born 1941, from her paternal grandmother...

"Don't confuse love and pity."

"This was just after my freshman year in college, as I tried to decide whether to commit to a long-term relationship with a moody young man. He was brilliant but later diagnosed as manic-depressive. I did break up with him, but not without guilt. I still confuse the two feelings. Even though my grandma warned me, I think she believed women should 'prop up' their men. I married vulnerable men, men like my father, an alcoholic—a recovering alcoholic with imagination and intelligence—but very serious problems."

Born 1949, from Mother...

"Your body is a cathedral."

"I was about fourteen when we were sitting in the living room, and she must have been feeling worried. But honestly, what I was thinking was, does that mean a man should take off his hat?

Now I think it's bullshit from her generation. I recognized exploring sexuality wasn't one of her priorities for me or for herself, and I gained some insight into why her life has been so full of conflict. I don't think she has ever accepted her sexuality, and I know it has been hard for the women of my generation in my family to accept theirs. We have tried, however.

Born 1928, from Grandmother...

"Don't be giggly. People will think you're simple-minded or loose (easy)."

"She warned of this anytime she felt it was appropriate, but I thought it as a silly, old-fashioned idea. Now that I'm older, I agree with her."

"She also warned …"

"Never trust a man."

"I thought that was silly, too, until I didn't."

Marlis Manley

Born 1959, from Mother…

"Boys always call the girls; you're not supposed to call the boy."

"This was in reference to dating, and I tended to disagree, even though I didn't press the issue. But when boys said they'd call and didn't, it caused me to distrust them, and I was 'unable' to call to find out what happened. Now I feel it's okay to call the opposite sex for a date."

Born 1959, from Mother and Father…

"Just do your best; that's all anyone can ask of you."

"They said this whenever I faced fear-inducing personal performances or tests. It was comforting to be reminded they were measuring me against my own abilities and not someone else's. I pass this on to my students here at the university, and it still helps me keep my own performance in various activities in perspective in relation to my self-esteem."

Born 1960, from Mother...

"Girls can't go camping without an adult."

"I waited until I was 14 to ask to go camping with my friends because my brothers never got to go out alone until they were 14, but I was told no and thought it was very unfair. And sexist. And probably wise. Even today, I'm afraid to go camping without an adult."

Born 1928, from Grandmother...

"Men will use you and then leave you, and no one else will want you."

"She said this from time to time, and I thought she was being old-fashioned and silly. Now I believe it."

Born 1951, from Mother and Father...

"Go into teaching so if your husband gets to be out of work, you'll have something to fall back on."

"I heard this all my growing-up years. It sounded logical since I'd be married someday. Now that I'm older, I think it's lousy advice. I hated teaching and didn't get married until age 27. I'd never thought of myself as not getting married and having kids, so I had a lot of 'brain wave modification' to do. I wish I'd have been raised to see myself as a complete person instead of as support personnel for a man. Real life was a shocker. I still struggle at times. "

[Editor's note: When I was teaching at Iowa State, I had dinner with my birth father, who quoted Woody Allen to me: "Those who can, do. Those who can't teach. Those who can't teach, teach gym." He was a genius engineer, so I was never sure he knew it was supposed to be a joke.]

Born 1932, from Mother ...

"A really intelligent woman never lets a man know she is smarter than he is."

"I actually believed it was not 'OK' to do better academically than boys. Now, I see that advice as a manipulation to place all responsibility on the other gender, which I really don't want to give them anyway. I think I still tend toward very cryptic expressions of opinions so that I get a chance to express them, but unless encouraged, I do not reveal my thinking/knowledge base when men are present."

Born 1932, from Mother ...

"What will people think, or what will the neighbors say?"

"I heard this when I stayed out late on dates, wore clothing she didn't find appropriate, etc. I thought my parents cared a lot more about what others said than they did about my welfare. I was careful never to pass that along to my daughters, but I still feel insecure about clothing, appearance, and others' opinions, and this really irritates me—that I can't let it go."

Born 1926, from Father …

"You will never get a job in anthropology! I would rather you think of teaching or business."

"It was my sophomore year in college, and my father wanted me to have an education in case I should become a widow or 'worse,' not so much for my own purposes. I was concerned he might be right, even though it was the only career interest I had. Since teaching or business was out of the question for me, we compromised on social work, which was a budding field at the time. At age 42, I returned to graduate school and got a degree in anthropology—which fulfilled a void in my life of unmet needs and aspirations."

Born 1923, from Mother ...

"Put this cloth in your panties each month when you see this."

"I was scared and wanted to know more, but I could tell I wasn't going to get it from my mother. I was not too shy, so I asked my friends. One friend's dad was a doctor, so we sneaked into his office, got out his books, and found out about periods and other things for ourselves.

I got along okay, but I always wished my mother could have been able to sit and talk with me about my body and its functions and about sex, etc. She was brought up very straight-laced (she didn't know how long it took to have a baby until her first pregnancy), so she didn't know how to talk to her girls about such things.

Peers know or find out a lot of things, and I did talk to my older sisters after I had some knowledge and wouldn't appear dumb to them. I did resolve to do better with my own girls (I had only one), and I was freer than my mom. But I also felt grateful to the Kotex company for having the films the school presented to the girls."

Born 1969, from Father …

"My father would always ask me to wear a dress when we went out to eat at a relative's or had relatives over for a celebration."

"I hated wearing skirts. My three brothers did not have to, so I didn't think it was fair that I had to. I wanted to be a boy anyway, and a skirt only made me more feminine. I know I can please my father by wearing a skirt, but it has made me resentful. Now, when he asks me to do something he knows I do not want to do, I deliberately do the opposite."

Born 1968, from Father's friend …

"The two places for a woman are in the kitchen and in the bedroom."

"I had asked my dad's friend what he thought of women working outside the home. I was about 15 at the time. I thought his answer was funny. Now we all know women have as much right to work outside the home as men."

Born 1951, from Mother …

"If someone picks on you at school, they're only doing it because they like you. You should turn the other cheek."

"At the time, it made me feel more noble—even though I was bruised most of the time. But it was really lousy advice. I should have been trained to stand up for myself. Kids don't pick on you because they like you; they pick on you because they're mean. I still have trouble being assertive. And I have trouble teaching my six-year-old son to stand up for himself."

Born 1924, from Mother ...

"If your boyfriend or fiancé makes any demands on you before marriage, don't give in, but send him to a brothel instead."

"I believed it and followed the advice. The man was very hurt, and I quickly realized that at least the second part of the advice was wrong and passé for my generation. I still believe in not giving in at 16. Married or not, the first time is very important for a woman. It should never be undertaken as part of 'his' education,' but should happen only if she genuinely loves the man. Some people have the maturity for such a love under the age of 20, and some do not until later. I have tentatively listened to parents, peers, and friends in matters of love, but always to my own voice first, which I learned to trust. Thus, I saved myself many disappointments."

Born 1944, from Mother ...

"Pretty is as pretty does."

"When a good deed was in order, or a kindness needed to be extended, she said this. I believed her but wondered if the world would agree. The older I got, the more I agreed. Kindness goes a long way in a friendship or any relationship. Selfishness, snobbery, jealousy, inflated ego—all are ugly traits. I've shared the saying with my daughters."

[Editor's note: I wonder what the equivalent saying would be for boys.]

Born 1945, from Father ...

"Put on lipstick before you go out."

"Whenever I was going out on social occasions, he told me to do this, but I thought it was nonsense. I still wear less make-up than most people, mostly because I don't want to be bothered. However, I do think I look better when I wear it."

Born 1945, from Father ...

"You have to share what you were apportioned—your intelligence and all your material goods. You have both, not because you deserved them, simply because they were given to you as a gift. You were just lucky."

"In my first-grade class, there was a girl from a very low-income family, and she did not have many books. I realized my mom was right, and I've never forgotten that what I have is a gift, and I should treasure and value it."

[Editor's note: Not where I thought this was going.]

Born 1954, from Mother …

"You have to protect the male ego."

"When I was in grade school, I asked for a larger allowance by pointing out that my brother, who was a year older, got more money and wasn't required to help out around the house (wash dishes, etc.) as much. That was her response. I thought it was garbage, and I still do. However, I still think of men as more emotionally fragile—I mean, I really believe they aren't as emotionally mature as women (fragile ego and all).

Born 1951, from Grandmother...

"If you sing at the table, you're crazy."

"When I would try to sing at the table, she would say this, frustrating me. I thought it was a strange way to insist on polite conversation. When alone and singing, I wonder what crazy really is and am I?"

Born 1951, from Mother and Grandmother...

"Men are animals. All they want is sex."

"I heard this when they were talking about my father (my parents were divorced). It made me fearful, and I know sometimes it's true. I was left with a mistrust of a man's motivation for closeness."

Born 1948, from Mother...

"Always have the table set when the men come in for dinner, even if it's not ready. They'll think something is coming."

"This was when dinner was going to be late, and I thought it was a bother, but then the table had to be set eventually." I can see now that it was probably good advice—an innocuous kind of deception. Unfortunately, I'm rarely organized enough to have the table set in advance. Besides, my husband cooks dinner as often as I do, so he knows how long it will be before things are ready. I often think about it, though, when my kids keep asking, 'How long before dinner?"

Born 1958, from Mother...

"Why can't you be more like your sister (meaning outgoing, popular, good grades in school)?"

"She said this when I was refusing to sing a solo in junior high choir, and I thought it stunk! (You need to know the sister was four years younger and Mommy's little pet angel who could do no wrong. You should never ever compare one child to another. All people are different. Don't force them to be what they aren't. I still don't like my sister."

Born 1954, from Father...

"If you want to do something unusual in your life, go ahead and do it. You'll find out it's not half as great as you thought it would be, but that way, you won't regret not having done it."

"I wanted to teach horseback and trail riding at YMCA camp in the Ozarks, and I was surprised by his advice but thought it was good. I still look at new situations with that view in mind. I realize that he regretted not having tried some new experiences."

Born 1968, from Mother...

"All guys are buttholes."

"I'd had a fight with my boyfriend, and that was mom's way of showing support. I actually believed it then and still do, but I also understand that men are different from women, and

I've gotten to understand them better."

Born 1943, from Mother…

"Stand up straight, don't slouch, pull in that tummy, sit up straight, walk tall, hold your head up, etc."

"I heard this often, especially when trying on clothes or having skirts hemmed, and I know it's important to look better, and posture is one of the first things I notice. However, some years later, a doctor informed me I had scoliosis, probably from age 12 or so, and one hip is one inch higher—making my efforts at standing straight fruitless. If Mom had had a doctor check me, the problem might have been correctable. Now I just stiffen my back when I pass a mirror, her criticism still in my ears, and the pain in my back."

Born 1943, from Grandmother…

"Marry young and don't date many different guys. People will think you're tough."

"I found this amusing, and I was amazed at how accepting of their situation women used to be—never seeming to question anything and appearing happy, and also at how talkative about sex she was. I think affectionately of her advice—some of which applies and some that doesn't—and it makes for good family stories and a sense of heritage with my kids. She's such a favorite in our memories."

Born 1960, from Mother…

"Curl your hair, put on some make-up, and quit being so emotional."

"That advice was just wrong for the person I was and am,

but it was practical advice when dating. I actually think that message states to me how I should try to be what I'm not, devaluing who I am, and I hope I don't pass this on to my friends and family. I'm uncomfortable with my appearance and expressing my feelings."

Born 1923, from Father...

"You girls have to be tough to survive in this world—so be like a man, and you will make me proud."

"This was said to me and my three sisters when our only brother was very ill (in bed for nearly six months). Since he wasn't able to 'be the man,' Dad expected the girls to be. I thought nearly everything my dad said was okay, and I had deep love and respect for him. As I look back, it was good advice. My husband died when he was 28, and I was 26. The 'Be tough' advice got me through some very hard times and enabled me to show a good example of courage and determination to my three children. Being tough is not being less feminine or being rude or bossy—it is more of an inner toughness."

Born 1936, from Mother...

"Don't teach elementary school. Anybody can do that."

"That was my mother's advice when I was choosing a college major, and I didn't believe her, but I got a double major, one to please her, one to please me. I believe an elementary teacher should be one of the most talented, well-educated persons possible. It takes such skill and compassion, and not just anyone can do it. I've tried a number of jobs. None has been more rewarding than teaching elementary school. I am glad of the varied education I've had and enjoyed all areas of study and all the jobs I've had."

Born 1960, from Mother...

"If you don't think you can, then you won't."

"Those words were worth careful consideration when I was going through a career change and was feeling a bit lost. It's good advice and supports self-determination. It helped build my confidence and helped me realize how essential it is to believe in yourself."

Part Four: Say What?

"We might as well be drunk as the way we are."

Born 1930, from an aunt (maiden lady, teetotaler)…

"We might as well be drunk as the way we are."

"When wine or spirits were offered in a social situation, she'd make this joke."

Born 1940, from Mother…

"I'd be ashamed of myself in the dark."

"I heard this when I severely disobeyed, but what difference does the dark make?"

Born 1930, from Mother…

"You'll never see it on a trottin' horse."

"She said this when our clothes weren't as snazzy as we wished."

Born 1930, from Grandmother…

"There, there, little darlin'."

"When anyone needed comforting, I found it interesting she didn't say, 'It's all right' or 'It'll be okay.' It was just pure raw comfort."

Born 1911, from Mother…

"That would sound better if someone else said it."

"When I bragged about myself, thinking she would be proud of me. I think it's good advice. I never brag."

Born 1946, from Mother…

"An empty barrel makes a lot of noise."

"When I told her what other kids had said, she'd say that, and I guess it's a good metaphor. Experience has taught me there are a lot of other empty barrels in the world. I grew up placing great value on reserve and guilt. I was not very well prepared for the world, living in the world."

Born 1938, from Mother…

"If it had teeth, it'd bite you."

"It made me mad, but it appeared true, and now whenever I look for things, I look two or three times because I think perhaps I'm just not seeing them."

[Editor's note: Could be genetic. On The Cosby Show, the mother and grandmother jokingly discussed writing a new bride's guide for living with a man. Chapter three would be 'Where's my?'.

Born 1958, from Father...

"Tuna casserole is nasty."

"That was his warning to Mother not to make it, so I accepted it as a truism. I steadfastly avoid tuna casserole—and I do not own any albums by the rock group, 'Hot Tuna.'"

Born 1957, from Mother...

"Sometimes, I don't think he has enough sense to pound sand into a rat hole."

"My Mom used to get disgusted with my brother's lack of judgment. It's a good saying to use at work."

Born 1951, from Mother...

"I never forgive, and I never forget."

"Upon returning home from a trip, my parents found the house a mess because of a party my brother had had. I was away at college. My brother told me what Mom had said. I don't know if she meant it, but it indicated how upset she was. From that point on, I have been careful with what I say and do around her."

[Editor's note: My stepfather told me that Mom once said if he did something 'wrong,' he wouldn't know how or even when, but she would get even. I doubt she meant it—she was a great tease—but as threats go, that's a gem.]

Born 1932, from Grandmother...

"He acts like the south end of a northbound horse. And why are there so many more horses' asses than there are horses?"

"This was when she was drawing attention to someone's stupid behavior. I've adopted these phrases for my own collection of 'wise sayings."

Born 1932, from Mother...

"Be kind to your web-footed friend."

"Whenever I engaged in ill behavior towards another person, especially strangers and/or minorities, she would say this, but I didn't get it. Now I realize it's sage advice to avoid discrimination in speech or behavior. I guess that's how I learned tolerance towards all kinds of people and developed a caring attitude.”

Born 1939, from Mother…

“Honesty is like good wine. Its benefits improve with age!”

“Dad used to say this often as just another rule to follow. I’ve passed it on to my children.”
[Editor’s note: I’m still pondering this.]

Born 1926, from Mother…

“A nod is as good as a wink to a blind horse.”

“She meant if you were trying to get something across to someone and it didn’t seem to register, it was useless to keep going.”

Born 1947, from Mother…

"Don't tell a lie, or you'll get a pimple on your tongue."

"She'd say it if someone got a sore on their tongue. It was strong enough of a warning that I believed she was right, and I still can't lie to her."

Born 1930, from Mother…

"The deed's been done, the child is born. Let's name him Ezry."

"This refers to when a decision is finally made, and it's time to look forward, not backward. I was shocked the first time she said that to me; I was a young adult still in the grips of the unacceptability of unwed folk having babies.

[Editor's Note: I remember hearing this when I was quite

young, visiting some of my Great Grandma Hattie's friends, and what I was most struck by was the name Ezra.]

Born 1964, from religion teacher…

"If God is all-powerful, can he make a rock so big that he himself can't lift it?"

"This was in Sunday school, and I was thoroughly confused. I'm still confused."

[Editor's Note: Me too.]

Born 1930, from Mother…

"If I had time, I'd faint."

"Mother's response when she heard some surprisingly good news of some minor accomplishment of ours. I use it myself."

Marlis Manley

Born 1926, from Father…

"People are part monkey, part hyena, and part leopard."

"When I first heard it, I thought it might be relevant, but now it seems a tad pessimistic."

Born 1948, from Father…

"You can never tell which way a frog will jump by just looking at it."

"When some outcome was in doubt, and there were many opinions on what was going to happen, Dad would pull this out, and you can't argue with it. If it had any effect, perhaps it's that I don't jump to conclusions?"

Born 1933, from Grandmother...

"Don't ever read anything you don't want to remember."

"On visiting her for the first time in about ten years, I commented that it was great she could read at 95. I thought her remark was funny with some wisdom. I think of her whenever I pick up a magazine or book with little or no socially redeeming value."

Born 1940, from Mother...

"You will have to live with a sore ass if you sit on a hot stove."

"Mother did not approve of my dating practices when I was a teenager. I was kind of shocked that my church-going (WASP) mother would use that sort of language. I granted her point, but she could have used a better choice of words

94

for the message."

[Editor's note: Could this be a euphemism for you know what? Asking for a friend.]

Final Thoughts

While putting this book together, I received invaluable assistance from one of the younger set—i.e., a man who spent his childhood in *this* century. He passed along a brand new (to me) excellent truism.

"Sometimes being quiet is the most difficult thing to do."

"My mother said this to me after I argued with a friend. I said some things to him I shouldn't have. It made me realize that in the heat of the moment, it's hard to stay silent. We say things we don't mean, and our words can harm people around us."

I hope you've enjoyed these stories of people sharing life's lessons, found words of wisdom here that have resonated for you personally, and had some laughs. Sometimes, that's the best kind of sharing.

About the Author

Marlis Manley Broadhead, a former college instructor of all forms of written communication except Braille, has award-winning short stories and poems in literary magazines—including *Kansas Quarterly, Mikrokosmos, Crosscurrents, and Kansas Women Writers.* Her historical novel, TROPHY GIRL, published by Black Rose Writing, was awarded the William Faulkner second prize in 2018.

Marlis Manley

While still living in Wichita, her hometown, where she earned her MFA with Distinction in Creative Writing, she started a Learning Skills Center at the Vo-Tech School for refugees from the Vietnam War—located on the campus of her *alma mater,* Wichita High School East.

In 1981, she and her family moved to Iowa State University, where she taught Business Communication and worked as an editor for *Better Homes and Garden's* building department.

Thanks to the development of fax machines, she took that editing job to northern California. There, she also taught a variety of writing classes at College of the Redwoods in Fort Bragg, founded the *Mendocino Coast Writers Conference* (still going), helped start a homeless shelter (a disaster eventually), helped form the *Mendocino Coast Children's Fund* (still thriving), and steered Fort Bragg Center for the Arts—a public showcase for local artists, who outnumber regular folks out there, five to one.

Back home in Kansas (by way of Stillwater, Oklahoma, and Chicago), she lives with her husband, Glenn, and a small menagerie on a modest horse ranch just south of

Kansas City, where she is working on her third novel and serializing stories on Amazon Kindle Vella in the brave new world of social media.

Thank you for choosing Is That Your Mother Calling? *If you enjoyed it, won't you please tell your friends and leave a review on Amazon, Barnes and Noble, or wherever you made your purchase?*

For updates on upcoming publications and giveaways, sign up for my newsletter, "Musings & Mirth," at https://marlisbroadhead.com. You can find my William Faulkner award-winning novel Trophy Girl *in print and audio at all major booksellers. It's inspired by the racing careers of my two fathers, both named Frank. For their (conflicting) advice to me on "the birds and the bees," go*

to My Fathers Frank and the Birds and the Bees.

If you've received or given advice that has a story with it and would like to share, please send it to marlis.broadhead@gmail.com with your year of birth, gender, who gave it to you, why, and how it's impacted your life. I'm gathering entries for a 21st-century follow-up.

My two cents: first, do no harm, and leave it better than you found it.

www.ingramcontent.com/pod-product-compliance
Lightning Source LLC
Chambersburg PA
CBHW041337120726
48005CB00014B/2299